Language Literacy Lessons

Words & Vocabulary

Elementary

by Imogene Forte

Incentive Publications, Inc.
Nashville, Tennessee

Illustrated by Gayle S. Harvey
Cover Art by Rebecca Rüegger
Edited by Jean K. Signor

ISBN 0-86530-571-4

PRINTED IN THE UNITED STATES OF AMERICA
www.incentivepublications.com

Table of Contents

Appendix **75**

HOW TO USE THIS BOOK

Achieving language literacy is a major benchmark in the education of every student in today's classrooms. Without reading, writing, speaking, and listening literacy the process of learning becomes increasingly difficult and the limits placed on academic achievement become more entrenched and solidified each year.

In the information saturated and technology dependent world of today, it is especially important for children to gain and be able to make meaningful use of the skills associated with language literacy at an early age. Success in content-based studies such as Math, Social Studies, and Science, and even in enrichment fields including Art, Music, and Literature are highly dependent on language literacy proficiency. With strong language skills, a student's academic future has fewer bounds and individual goals, expectancies, and dreams stand a better chance of being realized. It was with respect for the importance of achieving a high level of language literacy for every student that the Language Literacy Lessons Series was developed.

The purpose of *Language Literacy Lessons: Words & Vocabulary, Elementary* is to help students achieve the desired literacy milestone through reinforcement of key language skills. The activities in this book have all been designed to provide student practice of essential words and vocabulary skills. A skills checklist on page 10 details the skills covered. This skills checklist has been carefully gleaned from attention to research related to language while specific skills associated with each lesson are correlated to the age appropriate language literacy checklist.

Through the use of the lessons in this book, students will be advancing individual language literacy skills while working toward national standards! For help in lesson planning, an easy-to-use matrix on pages 8 and 9 presents National Language Arts Standards correlations for each lesson in the book.

Not only are the activities correlated to essential literacy skills and National Language Arts Standards, they are imaginative and their open-ended nature will prove to be engaging and of high-interest to students. Student creativity is tapped through intriguing situations to write about, interesting characters to read about, and captivating illustrations to inspire thoughtful student responses.

As language literacy skills improve, increased levels of overall school success will be readily apparent. Language literacy enables students to set achievable goals to go wherever their interests take them and to embark joyfully on a lifelong journey of learning!

STANDARDS MATRIX

STANDARD	ACTIVITY PAGE
Standard 1: Students read a wide range of print and nonprint text to build an understanding of texts, of themselves, and of the cultures of the United States and the world, to acquire new information, to respond to the needs and demands of society and the workplace, and for personal fulfillment. Among these texts are fiction and nonfiction, classic and contemporary works.	28, 72
Standard 2: Students read a wide range of literature from many periods in many genres to build an understanding of the many dimensions (e.g., philosophical, ethical, aesthetic) of human experience.	45, 46, 54, 55, 65
Standard 3: Students apply a wide range of strategies to comprehend, interpret, evaluate, and appreciate texts. They draw on their prior experience, their interactions with other readers and writers, their knowledge of word meaning and of other texts, their identification strategies, and their understanding of textual features (e.g., sound-letter correspondence, sentence structure, context, graphics).	16, 19, 23, 31, 32, 33, 40, 42, 43, 47, 53
Standard 4: Students adjust their use of spoken, written, and visual language (e.g., conventions, style, vocabulary) to communicate effectively with a variety of audiences for a variety of purposes.	15, 36, 37, 48, 49, 50, 58, 62, 71
Standard 5: Students employ a wide range of strategies as they write and use different writing process elements appropriately to communicate with different audiences for a variety of purposes.	14, 20, 21, 29, 57, 74
Standard 6: Students apply knowledge of language structure, language conventions (e.g., spelling and punctuation), media techniques, figurative language, and genre to create, critique, and discuss print and non-print texts.	12, 13, 17, 18, 25, 26, 27, 34, 41, 51

Standards for the English Language Arts, by the International Reading Association and the National Council of Teachers of English, Copyright 1996 by the International Reading Association and the National Council of Teachers of English. Reprinted with permission.

Language Literacy Lessons / Words & Vocabulary Elementary
Copyright ©2002 by Incentive Publications, Inc.
Nashville, TN.

STANDARDS MATRIX

STANDARD	ACTIVITY PAGE
Standard 7: Students conduct research on issues and interests by generating ideas and questions, and by posing problems. They gather, evaluate, and synthesize data from a variety of sources (e.g., print and non-print texts, artifacts, people) to communicate their discoveries in ways that suit their purpose and audience.	42, 56, 63, 66, 70
Standard 8: Students use a variety of technological and informational resources (e.g., libraries, databases, computer networks, video) to gather and synthesize information and to create and communicate knowledge.	19, 22, 73
Standard 9: Students develop an understanding of and respect for diversity in language use, patterns, and dialects across cultures, ethnic groups, geographic regions, and social roles.	55, 62
Standard 10: Students whose first language is not English make use of their first language to develop competency in the English language arts and to develop understanding of content across the curriculum.	39, 67
Standard 11: Students participate as knowledgeable, reflective, creative, and critical members of a variety of literacy communities.	22, 52, 60, 61, 64, 68, 69
Standard 12: Students use spoken, written, and visual language to accomplish their own purposes (e.g., for learning, enjoyment, persuasion, and the exchange of information).	24, 30, 38, 44, 59, 67

Language Literacy Lessons / Words & Vocabulary Elementary
Copyright ©2002 by Incentive Publications, Inc.
Nashville, TN.

Standards for the English Language Arts, by the International Reading Association and the National Council of Teachers of English, Copyright 1996 by the International Reading Association and the National Council of Teachers of English. Reprinted with permission.

SKILLS CHECKLIST

	SKILL	PAGE
	Recognizes and uses proper nouns	12
	Knows and uses vowel rules	13
	Knows and uses consonant sounds, blends, and rules	13, 14, 15
	Recognizes and understands functions of word endings and letter combinations that can be combined to form or change the sounds and/or meanings of words	16, 17, 18
	Knows and can use phonetic symbols	19
	Demonstrates skills in vocabulary extension	20, 21, 22, 23
	Knows and can use rules for syllabication	24
	Can use contractions and abbreviations	25, 26, 27, 28
	Can use compound words	29, 30, 31
	Can discriminate between words that look similar but are pronounced differently	32
	Recognizes and uses word association	33
	Recognizes and uses plurals	34
	Can use picture clues	36
	Can use context clues	37
	Can define words by classification or function	38, 39, 40, 41, 42
	Uses precise words	43
	Recognizes word relationships	44
	Can understand multiple meanings of a given word	45, 47
	Recognizes and can use common antonyms and homonyms for familiar words	48, 49, 50
	Recognizes and can use homophones	51
	Demonstrates vocabulary development skills	52
	Recognizes and can use analogies	53
	Can associate words with feelings	54, 55, 56
	Exhibits word sensitivity	57
	Can form sensory impressions	58, 59, 60
	Can interpret figurative and idiomatic expressions	61
	Can interpret sensations and moods suggested by words	62, 63
	Can recognize and use descriptive words	64, 65, 66, 67, 68, 69, 70
	Demonstrates word knowledge	71, 72
	Exhibits word appreciation skills	73, 74

Word Recognition and Usage Skills

Special Delivery

All the postal workers in Noun Town, U.S.A. are attending a postal conference. It's your job to help sort and deliver the mail on time.

Circle all of the proper nouns that are *not* capitalized but *should be* capitalized.

1. jean's letter to Jason must be delivered today.

2. Mr. Shibley's birthday card to his wife, debbie, needs additional postage.

3. monty wants to buy a stamp with a picture of the statue of liberty on it.

4. The address should read, "mrs. J. streams 607 S. brook st., Cleveland, Ohio 27205."

5. There are ten special delivery letters in julie's mailbox.

6. When will this letter from Australia be delivered to blake?

7. Six branch post offices in noun town are closed for repairs.

8. mike received seven Christmas cards from friends around the country.

9. Did you tell margaret that the first class mail will be late today?

10. In spite of her pleading, the mail for emily's street continues to be late.

11. No package will be delivered on thanksgiving day.

12. Mail for the gulf coast is on time for the first time since december.

13. She will pick up her mail next tuesday.

14. The book about african tigers is too heavy to mail in a brown envelope.

15. postal service between cities in the united States of America is available.

Name: _____   Date: _____

| *Recognizing and Using Proper Nouns* |

Language Literacy Lessons / Words & Vocabulary Elementary
Copyright ©2002 by Incentive Publications, Inc.
Nashville, TN.

Under the Phonics Umbrella

Color all the consonant spaces in the umbrella yellow.
Color all the vowel spaces orange. (Color the rest of the picture as you wish.)
Circle all the **long U** sounds in the following sentence:

> Ursula Upchurch usually waited under the umbrella until
> her uncle unpacked his unused ukulele.

Name: _____

Date: _____

Recognizing Consonants and Vowels

The Great Consonant Case

Fill in the missing consonants. Circle or make a mark on each consonant in the magnifying glass as you use it in the paragraphs below.

I__ you work care__ully, you ca__ find the missin__ consonan__s right under Sly Sam t__e Sleuth's eyes. Cir__le a consonant whe__ you put it in its proper pla__e, and you will know __ot to go loo__ing for it a__ain.

Sly Sa__ has bee__ assigned __o the __reat Consonant Ca__e. Consonants __eep __isappearing in lar__e num__ers right ou__ of otherwise sensi__le sen__ences. More consonants are mis__ing eve__y day. The words are be__inning to __anic, and although Sly Sam is smar__ and __rave, even he is desperate. Ca__ you come to his re__cue?

Please hurry and repla__e the missing consonants to re__urn peace and __uiet to Sly Sam's world.

The one stray vowel and five leftover consonants create a message to you from Sly Sam. Write the message here:

" _____ !!"

Name: _____   Date: _____

Language Literacy Lessons / Words & Vocabulary Elementary
Copyright ©2002 by Incentive Publications, Inc.
Nashville, TN.

Silent Skyscraper

Begin at dot #1 and quietly pronounce the word.

If the word contains a silent consonant, find the next word in numerical order with a silent consonant, and draw a line between the two. (If the very next word does not contain a silent consonant, skip that word and proceed to the next one.)

Continue connecting words with silent consonants until the drawing is completed.

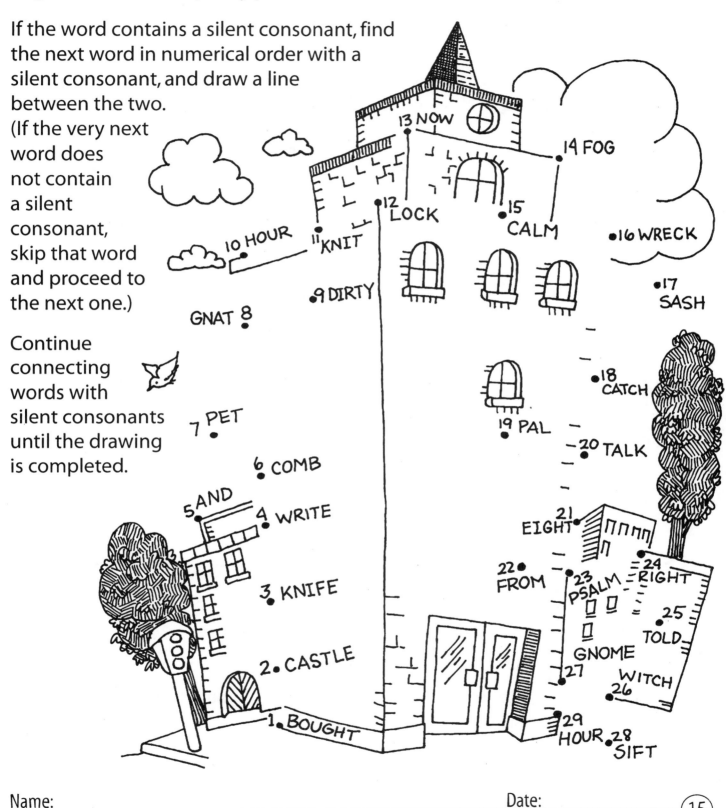

13 NOW
14 FOG
12 LOCK
15 CALM
16 WRECK
10 HOUR
11 KNIT
17 SASH
9 DIRTY
GNAT 8
18 CATCH
7 PET
19 PAL
20 TALK
6 COMB
5 AND
4 WRITE
21 EIGHT
24 RIGHT
22 FROM
23 PSALM
25 TOLD
3 KNIFE
GNOME
27
WITCH 26
2. CASTLE
1. BOUGHT
29 HOUR
28 SIFT

Name: Date:

Language Literacy Lessons / Words & Vocabulary Elementary   *Using Silent Consonants*
Copyright ©2002 by Incentive Publications, Inc.
Nashville, TN.

Is it "D" or "T"

When *-ed* is added to the end of a word but does not form a separate syllable, the *-ed* will sound like either a **D** or a **T**.

Read the words below.

Write the words with **D** ending sounds in the large **D** shape, and the words with **T** ending sounds in the large **T** shape .

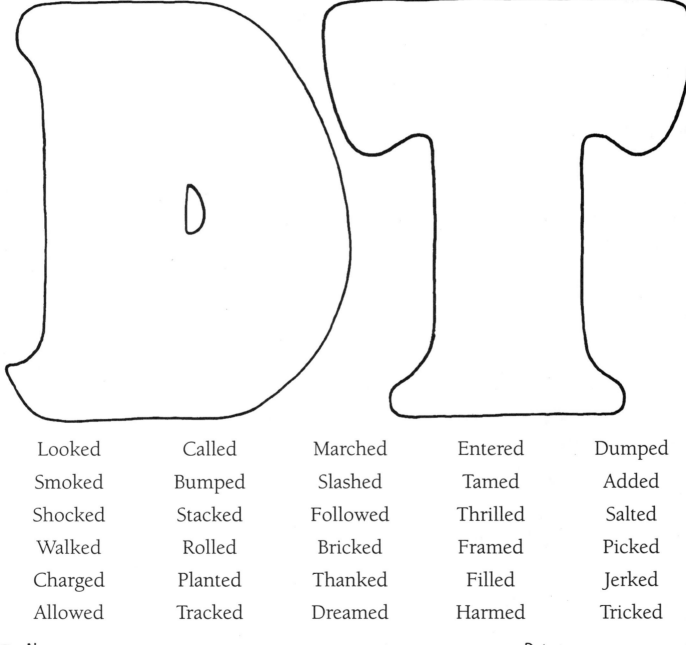

Looked	Called	Marched	Entered	Dumped
Smoked	Bumped	Slashed	Tamed	Added
Shocked	Stacked	Followed	Thrilled	Salted
Walked	Rolled	Bricked	Framed	Picked
Charged	Planted	Thanked	Filled	Jerked
Allowed	Tracked	Dreamed	Harmed	Tricked

Name: Date:

Language Literacy Lessons / Words & Vocabulary Elementary
Copyright ©2002 by Incentive Publications, Inc.
Nashville, TN.

Letter-ing

Read the words below and decide if the last letter in each word should be doubled or dropped before adding the *-ing* suffix. Write each new word ending with *-ing* in the correct letter boxes below.

hop	plan	time	sit	live	hope
come	wake	tap	swim	love	bat
grin	snore	strike	fan	trim	like

Double-Letter "ing" Words:

Dropped-Letter "ing" Words:

love

Name: _____   Date: _____

Language Literacy Lessons / Words & Vocabulary Elementary
Copyright ©2002 by INCENTIVE PUBLICATIONS, Inc.
Nashville, TN.

Recognizes and Understands Word Endings

Treasure Hunt

Long ago pirates left treasures untold on the ocean floor.
Find out about the searches some treasure hunters are doing to recover
these unfound treasures. Write the correct ending for each unfinished word
in the story. Use **ed, ing,** or **s.**

Find____ hidden treasure is not an easy task.

We search____ a long time before find____ the first one.

Suddenly we saw the open____ chest full of brilliant gem____ rest____ on the ocean's floor.

Jewel____ and gem____ of every description appear____ before our eye____.

Quickly, we rush____ straight ahead to claim the chest.

Imagine our surprise when the chest fail____ to move when we push____ and pull____ with all our strength.

In spite of our mighty move____ the chest remain____ in its original position.

Strain____ every muscle in our body we tried lift____ the chest upright.

Alas, our effort____ were in no way successful.

That chest filled with treasure____ untold was there to stay.

Name: _____   Date: _____

Recognizing and Understanding
Ineffectual Word Endings

Language Literacy Lessons / Words & Vocabulary Elementary
Copyright ©2002 by Incentive Publications, Inc.
Nashville, TN.

Phonics Foolers

A Phonics Fooler is a joke or rhyme written in phonetic notation. Translate this fooler by writing its standard spelling version on the lines beside it.

Yōō dōn't nēd ā rōō'-lər   _____

Tōō trăns-lāt' thĭs fōō'-lər   _____

Jŭst yōōz ôl yōō nō   _____

ə-bout' fŏn'-ĭks, ənd GŌ!   _____

Make up 3 Phonetic Foolers of your own, and write them in the spaces below. (Find the correct phonetic form for each word in a dictionary.)
Exchange papers with a classmate, and rewrite his or her Foolers in standard spelling. Then discuss your translations.

Name: _____   Date: _____   19

Word-Maker, Word-Maker!!

Look at each word in the word packages below.
Make 6 new words from each word by changing 1 letter at a time.
The first one is completed for you.

SOAP	SEAT	KITE	FOAM	PINT	LAKE
SOAK					
SOCK					
LOCK					
LOOK					
TOOK					
TOOL					

Name: _____   Date: _____
Demonstrating Skills in Vocabulary Extension
Language Literacy Lessons / Words & Vocabulary Elementary
Copyright ©2002 by Incentive Publications, Inc.
Nashville, TN.

The Magic Triangle Tangle

Morto the Magician had to use his magic wand to find 25 words that can be made from the letters in the word:

T R I A N G L E S

You can do it with just your pencil!
Write the 25 words you find on the lines below.

Note: No letter may be used more than 1 time in a word.

Name: _____   Date: _____

Language Literacy Lessons / Words & Vocabulary Elementary
Copyright ©2002 by Incentive Publications, Inc.
Nashville, TN.

Demonstrating Skills in Vocabulary Extension

Word Wizard

A "Word Wizard" is a person who uses new and colorful words regularly in speaking and writing.
Do you know someone who is a "Word Wizard?"
You can become a "Word Wizard," too!

The first thing you must do to become a "Word Wizard" is to fill this wizard's bag with colorful and exciting words.

The second thing you must do is complete the wizard's face and clothes to make him your own special wizard.

The third and most important requirement is to USE THE WORDS!

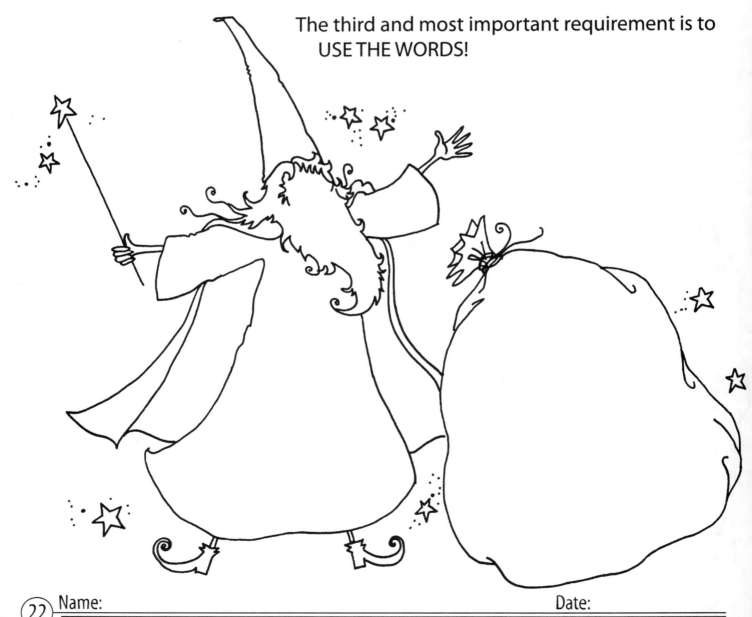

Name: _____   Date: _____

Demonstrating Skills in Vocabulary Extension   *Language Literacy Lessons / Words & Vocabulary Elementary*
Copyright ©2002 by Incentive Publications, Inc.
Nashville, TN.

Holiday Check-Up

Have you checked your holiday vocabulary lately?

Here's a little test to help you do just that.

1. Fill in the missing vowels in the words below.

2. Draw a line from the name of each holiday to the symbol that is associated with it.

Chr_stm_s

St. P_tr_ck's D_y

Th_nksg_v_ng

Ch_n_k_h

V_l_nt_n_s D_y

N_w Y__r's D_y

H_ll_w__n

Language Literacy Lessons / Words & Vocabulary Elementary
Copyright ©2002 by Incentive Publications, Inc.
Nashville, TN.

Demonstrating Skills in Vocabulary Extension

Syllables in Color

1. Color all the one-syllable words green.
2. Color all the two-syllable words orange.
3. Color all the three-syllable words brown.
4. Pronounce each word and count the total number of syllables in each color.

FINISH

ACT
LIKE
BUNDLE
TENNIS
ROT
WINDY
FIFTY
PROPERTY
DIRECTOR
TIRESOME
TWINKLE
PANIC
BIT
PONY
TRUTH
CARROT
HAPPINESS
DANGEROUS
BACON
WHO
VISIT
ONE
STRUGGLE
GALLOP
BALLOON
EARLY
POTTERY
FULL
ACTION
START

Name: _____

Date: _____

Recognizing Syllabication

Language Literacy Lessons / Words & Vocabulary Elementary

Write for Willie

Willie Worm forgot all about his homework. Now he is in real trouble.

Maybe you can help him out.

First read his word list.
Then write the correct abbreviation beside each term.

hour _____   centimeter _____

Drive _____   pound _____

Wednesday _____   Avenue _____

year _____   February _____

Doctor _____   kilogram _____

Mister _____   Road _____

feet _____   minute _____

paid _____   Yard _____

inch _____   liter _____

Sunday _____

mile _____

December _____

Name: _____

Date: _____

Language Literacy Lessons / Words & Vocabulary Elementary
Copyright ©2002 by Incentive Publications, Inc.
Nashville, TN.

Using Abbreviations

On Target

A contraction is formed when two words are joined together with an apostrophe in the middle.

Peter wants to become a great hunter.

Every day he practices with his bow and arrows. The letter targets he is shooting at are two words from which contractions can be made.

Draw an apostrophe arrow (/) through the letters you need to leave out to form a contraction. Write the contraction under the target. Say the contractions.

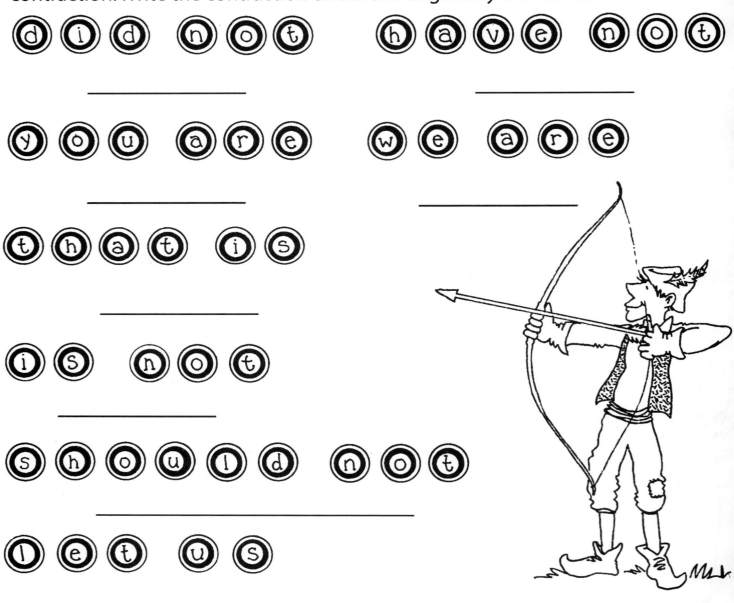

ⓓ ⓘ ⓓ ⓝ ⓞ ⓣ   ⓗ ⓐ ⓥ ⓔ ⓝ ⓞ ⓣ

_____   _____

ⓨ ⓞ ⓤ ⓐ ⓡ ⓔ   ⓦ ⓔ ⓐ ⓡ ⓔ

_____   _____

ⓣ ⓗ ⓐ ⓣ ⓘ ⓢ

_____

ⓘ ⓢ ⓝ ⓞ ⓣ

_____

ⓢ ⓗ ⓞ ⓤ ⓛ ⓓ ⓝ ⓞ ⓣ

_____

ⓛ ⓔ ⓣ ⓤ ⓢ

_____

Name:

Date:

Using Contractions

Language Literacy Lessons / Words & Vocabulary Elementary
Copyright ©2002 by Incentive Publications, Inc.
Nashville, TN.

Contraction Action

Question: What do fractions and contractions have in common?
  Answer: In math, two numbers are reduced to the lowest common denominator; in writing, two words are reduced into one shorter word.
Work a little contraction action with the words below.

I/will = _____

Does/not = _____

Could/not = _____

You/will = _____

They/are = _____

We/are = _____

I/am = _____

She/will = _____

Were/not = _____

Can/not = _____

There/is = _____

Was/not = _____

Where/is = _____

We/will = _____

You/are = _____

Has/not = _____

They/will = _____

Was/not = _____

Would/not = _____

Has/not = _____

Have/not = _____

Should/not = _____

Name: _____

Date: _____

Language Literacy Lessons / Words & Vocabulary Elementary
Copyright ©2002 by Incentive Publications, Inc.
Nashville, TN.

Using Contractions

Cast Off

Read the story of Emily and Julie's boat trip.
Then re-copy their story on the lines below, combining each pair of words in bold type to form a contraction.

Emily and Julie **could not** wait for the ship to sail. For days **they had** waited eagerly for this trip. Julie said to Emily, "**Do not** forget to be on deck as we embark. You **would not** want to miss seeing the anchor lifted. **That is** one of the most exciting parts of the trip." Julie looked at her watch and said, "**It is** only ten minutes until **we will** be pulling away from the shore. **Let us** find a good spot near the front of the ship where **you will** see everything. **I have** sailed once before and **I will** never forget the thrill of leaving port." Emily replied, "**I am** so excited. This is the trip of my dreams."

_____

_____

_____

_____

_____

_____

_____

_____

_____

_____

_____

_____

_____

Name: _____   Date: _____

Using Contractions

Language Literacy Lessons / Words & Vocabulary Elementary
Copyright ©2002 by Incentive Publications, Inc.
Nashville, TN.

Word Slide

The words below are compound words (two words which have been combined to create a new word).

Circle one part of each word. Draw a picture in the space provided to go with the word you circled. The first one is completed for you.

1. (FISH) HOOK
2. NOTEBOOK
3. STRAWBERRY
4. TEAKETTLE
5. SCREWDRIVER
6. CHALKBOARD
7. BUTTERFLY
8. STEPLADDER
9. FOOTBALL
10. COATTAIL
11. INKSTAND

1. _____
2. _____
3. _____
4. _____
5. _____
6. _____
7. _____
8. _____
9. _____
10. _____
11. _____

Name: _____   Date: _____

Using Compound Words

Compound Canvas

Circle all 15 compound words hidden in this framed canvas.

The words are listed horizontally (across) and vertically (up and down).

```
B  I  R  D  S  E  E  D  J  P  X  P
R  D  O  L  L  H  O  U  S  E  D  A
Q  C  X  P  L  A  Y  T  I  M  E  T
A  Z  D  B  G  O  L  D  F  I  S  H
B  A  L  L  R  O  O  M  E  N  T  W
R  O  P  W  E  G  B  J  Q  X  R  A
O  X  O  V  E  R  C  O  A  T  A  Y
O  B  A  R  N  Y  A  R  D  G  W  E
M  U  I  S  H  K  M  Y  S  R  B  B
S  C  Z  J  O  B  P  X  R  O  E  A
T  K  M  E  U  A  F  T  J  W  R  T
I  Q  X  V  S  O  I  H  K  N  R  H
C  A  D  H  E  J  R  K  X  U  Y  T
K  U  G  T  B  C  E  L  W  P  Z  U
X  C  A  R  D  B  O  A  R  D  H  B
```

Word List:

BALLROOM   STRAWBERRY   DOLLHOUSE

GREENHOUSE   PLAYTIME   GOLDFISH

CAMPFIRE   BATHTUB   BIRDSEED

BROOMSTICK   GROWNUP   PATHWAY

CARDBOARD   OVERCOAT   BARNYARD

Name: _____

Date: _____

Using Compound Words

Language Literacy Lessons / Words & Vocabulary Elementary
Copyright ©2002 by Incentive Publications, Inc.
Nashville, TN.

Compound Museum

Fill the museum walls with original compound word portraits.
The first one is completed for you—you do the rest!

TOENAIL

BUS BOY

GOLDFISH

COWGIRL

KNOT HOLE

PANCAKE

BALLROOM

WATCH TOWER

STREET CAR

List nine more compound words that could be
added to the museum collection.

1. _____   4. _____   7. _____

2. _____   5. _____   8. _____

3. _____   6. _____   9. _____

Name: _____   Date: _____   ③1

Using Compound Words

Word Clouds

wear
were

dare
dear

rare
rear

which
witch

their
there

flit
flat

ring
rang

sun
sum

could
cloud

Read the sentence sets below and decide which cloud's word pair goes with each sentence set. Write those words in the cloud beside each set. Then complete the sentences by writing in the correct words from the word pair selected.

I'd like to _____ the blue dress.
Where _____ you when I needed you?

This ground is as _____ as my hand.
Fireflies _____ to and fro at dusk.

She ordered her roast beef _____.
That _____ door should be fixed.

The desert _____ is unbelievably hot.
Adding two numbers together will give you the _____.

People go _____ to shop.
_____ dog disappeared.

The Halloween _____ looked scary.
_____ of these bikes do you like best?

I _____ go with you.
The dark _____ moved across the sky.

The telephone bell _____ loudly.
I heard the six o'clock bell _____.

Books are especially _____ to the librarian.
I _____ you to tell that story again.

Name: _____ Date: _____

Discriminating Between Words That Look Similar But Are Pronounced Differently

Language Literacy Lessons / Words & Vocabulary Elementary
Copyright ©2002 by Incentive Publications, Inc.
Nashville, TN.

Look–Alikes

1. Look carefully at the words in each row.
2. Cross out the word in each row that does not belong.
3. Draw a circle around the plural form of each word.

1. PENCILS	PENNY	PENCIL	8. BALL	BELLS	BELL
2. PAN	PAT	PANS	9. BUG	BAG	BUGS
3. TOE	TOES	TOP	10. ROCKS	RACK	ROCK
4. HATS	HOT	HAT	11. STRAPS	STRIP	STRAP
5. TREE	THREE	TREES	12. STRING	BRING	STRINGS
6. STOP	STOPS	STRIP	13. SHIP	SHIPS	SHOP
7. LETTER	LITTER	LETTERS	14. TAIL	TALE	TAILS

Name: _____   Date: _____

Language Literacy Lessons / Words & Vocabulary Elementary
Copyright ©2002 by Incentive Publications, Inc.
Nashville, TN.

Recognizing and Using Word Association /
Recognizing and Using Plurals

Two By Two

Old Noah built his ark.

When Noah built his ark, he brought the creatures in two by two.

Write the correct plural words from the list at the bottom of the page
to complete Noah's passenger list.

Bear _____   Rooster _____

Calf _____   Octopus _____

Deer _____   Sparrow _____

Fly _____   Elephant _____

Giraffe _____   Butterfly _____

Goose _____   Tiger _____

Mouse _____   Goat _____

Sheep _____   Dove _____

Wolf _____   Fox _____

Plurals:

calves	sheep	deer	sparrows	octopuses
wolves	geese	foxes	doves	tigers
flies	mice	roosters	elephants	
giraffes	bears	goats	butterflies	

Name: Date:

Recognizing and Using Plurals   *Language Literacy Lessons / Words & Vocabulary Elementary*
Copyright ©2002 by Incentive Publications, Inc.
Nashville, TN.

Word Comprehension and Sensitivity Skills

Rebus Race II

Try your luck at reading these rebuses. Sit where you can see a clock, and time yourself to see how long it takes you to figure out each one. Write each message on the line below its rebus, and record your time in the box.

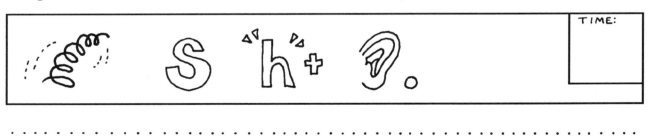

Date:

Using Picture Clues

Language Literacy Lessons / Words & Vocabulary Elementary

Should We or Shouldn't We?

Some words can be used more than one way in a sentence.

Read the sentences below.

Select the word from the word list that best fits each blank.

You will use the words more than once.

Use one of the words in a new sentence of your own to finish the story.

WORD LIST:

well   visit   cold

1. Is Grandmother feeling _____ now?

2. Tomorrow we hope to _____ her.

3. She always looks forward to our _____ .

4. Last week she had a _____ , so we didn't see her.

5. The weather outside is still _____ , and it might be easy to get sick.

6. _____ , maybe we should see her the next day instead.

7. _____

_____ .

Name: _____ Date: _____

Language Literacy Lessons / Words & Vocabulary Elementary
Copyright ©2002 by Incentive Publications, Inc.
Nashville, TN.

Using Context Clues

Apple Treats

Think about the many different ways we use apples. Add one extra word to each apple with a blank in the basket to make an apple treat.

If you think of more ways to use apples than there are apples in the basket, write in some extra ideas on the blank recipe card!

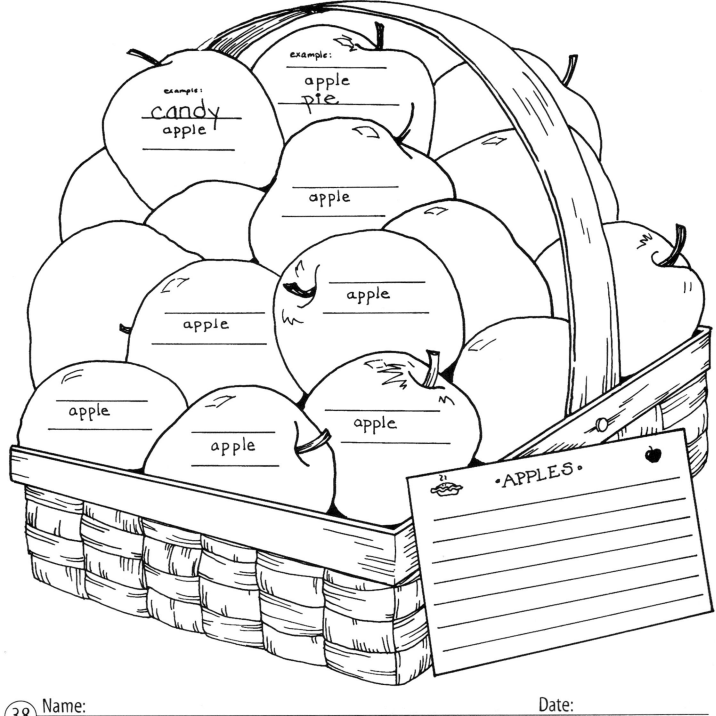

example: **candy** apple

example: **apple pie**

apple

apple

apple

apple

apple

apple

apple

• APPLES •

Name: Date:

Cinderella's Closet

Cinderella's closet is a mess! She's been so busy scrubbing floors and doing errands for her mean stepsisters that she has had little time for herself. Help her get ready to leave with the prince by marking out the item in each box that does not belong.

Name:

Date:

Language Literacy Lessons / Words & Vocabulary Elementary
Copyright ©2002 by Incentive Publications, Inc.
Nashville, TN.

Defining Words by Classification or Function

Mr. Mack Needs Help

Mr. Mack needs help.
The fruits and vegetables are mixed up.

Mark out the word in each basket that does not belong.

Draw three fruits in the empty fruit basket and
three vegetables in the empty vegetable basket.

Name: _____   Date: _____

Defining Words by Classification or Function   *Language Literacy Lessons / Words & Vocabulary Elementary*

Grammar Cracker Cake

Nouns and verbs and other parts of speech are recipe ingredients for sentences. They must be combined correctly so that a sentence will present a whole thought.

Read the recipe directions below.

Tell the part of speech of each underlined word by writing its name in the crossword puzzle.

CAKE ♥

GRAMMAR CRACKER CAKE

2 cups flour
1 cup milk
¼ tsp. salt
½ cup sugar
2 eggs
¼ box of crumbled graham crackers
2 tsp. cinnamon
2 tsp. baking powder
½ tsp. vanilla
¼ tsp. vanilla

DIRECTIONS

ACROSS:
1. First, <u>you</u> need a bowl.
2. Measure the ingredients CAREFULLY.
3. Mix ingredients well <u>AND</u> put them in a cake pan.
5. <u>Cook</u> at 350° for 25-30 minutes.

DOWN:
1. Take the cake out <u>OF</u> the oven and let cool.
2. Put a <u>DELICIOUS</u> icing on your cake.
4. Now your <u>CAKE</u> is ready to eat!

Name: _____   Date: _____

Language Literacy Lessons / Words & Vocabulary Elementary
Copyright ©2002 by Incentive Publications, Inc.
Nashville, TN.

Defining Words by Classification or Function

Classification Jumble

All of these packages came tumbling into the Classification Center. Please help restore order by drawing a line through the word in each package that does not belong. Write a classification word for the remaining words on the line below each package. (Use your dictionary if you need help.)

Write 3 words for each classification word listed on the boxes at the bottom of the page.

Example:

yacht
canoe
~~airplane~~
tug

boats

1
parka
jacket
muffler
shorts

2
poultry
pastry
parrot
pasta

4
encyclopedia
chalk
dictionary
atlas

5
castle
cabin
poncho
mansion

3
weasel
lily
angora
aardvark

6
kale
zucchini
apple
broccoli

8
New York City
Canada
England
Mexico

7
humid
freezing
sunny
growing

9
bucket pint
gallon quart

Plants

Toys

Fruits

Name: Date:

Defining Words by Classification or Function   Language Literacy Lessons / Words & Vocabulary Elementary
Copyright ©2002 by Incentive Publications, Inc.
Nashville, TN.

How's the Weather?

Write one complete sentence to give a weather report for each scene below.

1. _____
_____
_____
_____
_____

2. _____
_____
_____
_____
_____

3. _____
_____
_____
_____
_____

Name: _____   Date: _____   (43)

Language Literacy Lessons / Words & Vocabulary Elementary
Copyright ©2002 by Incentive Publications, Inc.
Nashville, TN.   *Using Precise Words*

On the Word Track

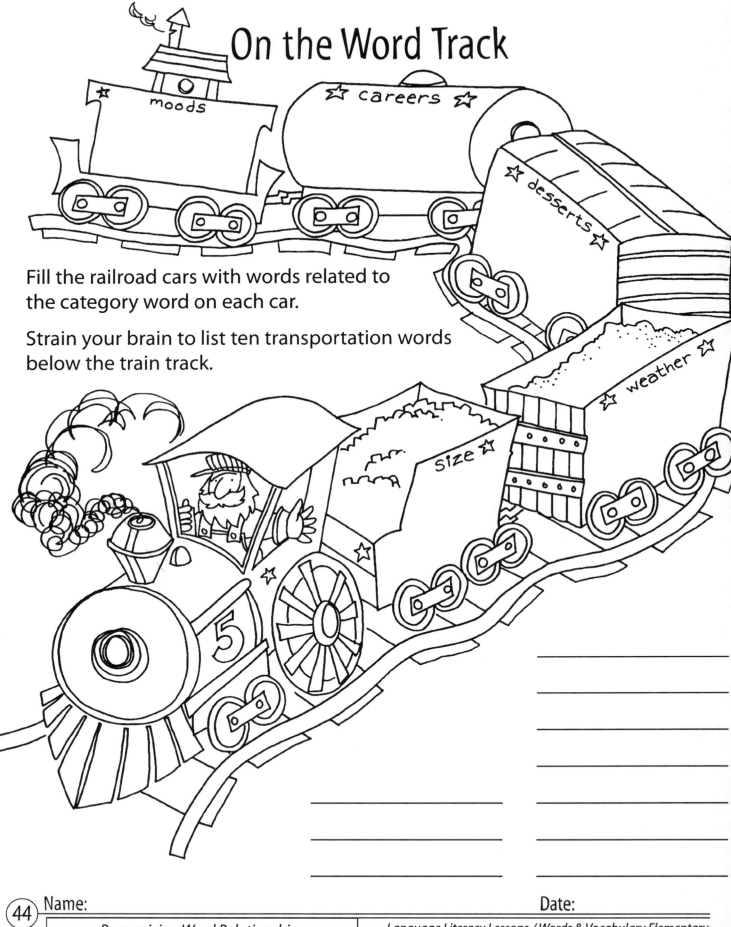

moods

☆ careers ☆

☆ desserts ☆

☆ weather ☆

size ☆

Fill the railroad cars with words related to the category word on each car.

Strain your brain to list ten transportation words below the train track.

_____

_____

_____

_____

_____

_____

Name: _____

Date: _____

Recognizing Word Relationships

Language Literacy Lessons / Words & Vocabulary Elementary
Copyright ©2002 by Incentive Publications, Inc.
Nashville, TN.

A Stormy Day

Read this paragraph carefully. Then, test your word knowledge by following the directions to complete the quiz.

1. The cold November wind whistled and moaned as it blew the dead weeds in the garden in front of the abandoned mansion. **2.** Wooden shutters banged noisily against the windows as the wintry wind tried to tear them off their half-broken hinges, and the tattered, rotting walls seemed to shudder as the icy fists of the storm beat against them. **3.** A driving rain poured from the cloudy, forbidding sky, turning the deserted garden into a sullen black lake that slowly and menacingly crept up to the crumbling concrete steps, while dead leaves floated like ghostly ships in the rising waters. **4.** A flashing yellow streak of lightning roared out of the sky and struck an old dead oak tree beside the house. **5.** The stricken tree quivered and rocked back and forth on its rotten roots. **6.** Slowly and silently it began to fall.

1. Circle the word that would best help you understand the meaning of the word **wind** in sentence 1 of the story.
   November
   whistled
   front

2. Circle the four words in sentence 2 that tell about weather.

3. Circle the word that means the same thing as **dead** as it is used in sentence 1.
   deceased
   dying
   old

4. Circle the word that means the opposite of **dead** as it is used in sentence 1.
   pretty
   withered
   living

5. Circle the word in sentence 3 that tells how the rain came from the sky.
   cloudy
   forbidding
   poured

6. Circle the word that best could be used to take the place of **silently** as it is used in sentence 6.
   noisily
   quietly
   quickly

Name:

Date:

Language Literacy Lessons / Words & Vocabulary Elementary
Copyright ©2002 by Incentive Publications, Inc.
Nashville, TN.

Understanding Multiple Meanings
of a Given Word

7. Circle the word that best describes how a child would feel in the stormy garden.

   carefree

   frightened

   contented

8. Draw a line under the four-word phrase in the paragraph that means the same thing as: *"It was raining cats and dogs."*

9. Circle the word that best describes the mood suggested in sentence 3.

   eerie

   joyful

   pensive

10. In sentence 3, *rain* is to *sky* as *plants* are to:

    bouquets

    earth

    catalogs

11. Circle the word that does not describe the oak tree in sentence 4.

    yellow

    old

    dead

12. Circle the word that could best be used to replace **tried** in sentence 2.

    roared

    attempted

    stooped

13. Circle the word that could best be used to replace **crumbling** in sentence 3.

    sloping

    eroding

    creeping

14. Circle the word that could correctly be added to the end of sentence 6.

    into

    forward

    beside

15. Write the two words from sentence 3 that have double letters.

    _____

    _____

16. Circle the word that could be used in a poem to rhyme with **yellow**.

    follow

    mellow

    lowly

Name: _____

Date: _____

Theme

Language Literacy Lessons / Words & Vocabulary Elementary
Copyright ©2002 by Incentive Publications, Inc.
Nashville, TN.

Star Light, Star Bright

Jan is a real word "sharpie".

She loves collecting words that have more than one meaning and using them to make word games.

Choose a word from the treasure chest below to help Jan complete the game board she is putting together.

The word selected must fit both meanings in the square.

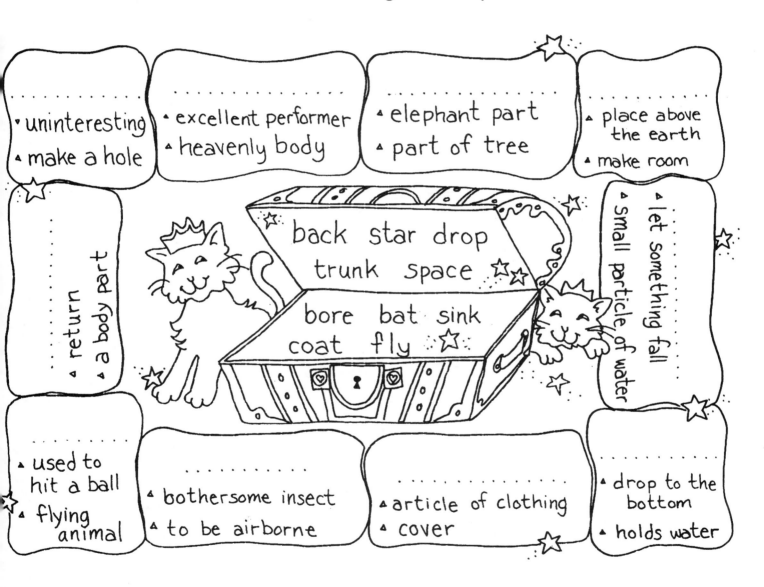

- uninteresting
- make a hole

- excellent performer
- heavenly body

- elephant part
- part of tree

- place above the earth
- make room

- return
- a body part

back   star   drop
trunk   space
bore   bat   sink
coat   fly

- let something fall
- small particle of water

- used to hit a ball
- flying animal

- bothersome insect
- to be airborne

- article of clothing
- cover

- drop to the bottom
- holds water

Name: Date:

Language Literacy Lessons / Words & Vocabulary Elementary
Copyright ©2002 by Incentive Publications, Inc.
Nashville, TN.

Understanding Multiple Meanings
of a Given Word

Up Homonym Hill

Jack and Jill went up Homonym Hill,
to find words that sounded the same.
Jack fell down, Jill heard a sound,
and said, "What a funny word game!"

Help Jack and Jill get back
up the hill. Select the
correct homonym from
the pail to write on each
stepping-stone.

Name: Date:

Recognizing and Using Homonyms
for Familiar Words

Language Literacy Lessons / Words & Vocabulary Elementary
Copyright ©2002 by Incentive Publications, Inc.
Nashville, TN.

Pair Up

Draw lines to connect the homonym pairs and the illustration that matches one of the words.
Underline the word that matches the illustration.

stare	cent	
scent	foul	
pair	stair	
plane	stake	
flower	waste	
waist	plain	
steak	flour	
fowl	pear	

Language Literacy Lessons / Words & Vocabulary Elementary
Copyright ©2002 by Incentive Publications, Inc.
Nashville, TN.

Recognizing and Using Homonyms
for Familiar Words

Name:

Date:

Marge's Word List

Marge loves to solve problems and work puzzles.

Today she is making a list of antonyms for a puzzle she plans to solve tonight.

An antonym is a word that means the opposite of another word.

Help Marge by writing an antonym for each word on her list.

1. clean _____

2. dark _____

3. sad _____

4. hot _____

5. bottom _____

6. ahead _____

7. short _____

8. small _____

9. brave _____

10. dull _____

11. sunny _____

12. generous _____

13. smile _____

14. night _____

15. fast _____

Name: _____   Date: _____

Recognizing and Using Common Antonyms for Familiar Words

Language Literacy Lessons / Words & Vocabulary Elementary
Copyright ©2002 by Incentive Publications, Inc.
Nashville, TN.

Homophone Hide and Seek

Homophones are words that sound alike but have different spellings and meanings.

To play Homophone Hide and Seek, find and color pictures of homophones for the following words hiding in the picture.

As you find and color each hidden picture, find the matching word in the word box.

Write the homophone on the line beside the matching word.

1. ate _____

2. bare _____

3. be _____

4. bough _____

5. carat _____

6. dough _____

7. flour _____

8. not _____

9. pale _____

10. pare _____

11. sale _____

12. tee _____

13. thrown _____

Name: _____

Date: _____

(51)

Recognizing and Using Homophones

Vacation Village

Write a story about Vicki and Victor's visit to Vacation Village.
In the story, use as many words beginning with the letter "V" as you can.
Use the word list below for help in writing your story.

_____

_____

_____

_____

_____

_____

_____

_____

_____

_____

Word List (Use your dictionary to find more.)

villa	vague	vagabond	vegetable	very
vacancy	villager	vehicle	vice	vinegar
voyage	valid	visitor	vain	vanguard

Name: _____   Date: _____

Demonstrating Vocabulary Development Skills   *Language Literacy Lessons / Words & Vocabulary Elementary*
Copyright ©2002 by Incentive Publications, Inc.
Nashville, TN.

The Crystal Ball

Look into the crystal ball. Find the word that completes each sentence. Write each word in the correct blank.

1. _____ is to **fairy** as **staff** is to **wizard**.

2. _____ is to **queen** as **pointed hat** is to **leprechaun**.

3. **Sing** is to **bird** as _____ is to **toad**.

4. **Tuffet** was to **Little Miss Muffet** as _____ was to **Humpty Dumpty**.

5. _____ is to a **princess** as **stomping** is to an **giant**.

6. A _____ was to **Mother Goose** as a **horse** is to a **knight**.

7. A **slate** was to **students long ago** as a _____ is to **students today**.

8. A **cup** is to a **saucer** as a _____ is to a **place mat**.

9. The **moon** is to **night** as the _____ is to **day**.

sun   goose   wand   wall   plate   croak   notebook   dancing   crown

Name: _____   Date: _____   (53)

Emotion Showcase

How do you show your emotions?

Write a complete sentence to tell how you act when:

…you are happy.

_____

_____

…you are sad.

_____

_____

…you are afraid.

_____

_____

…you are surprised.

_____

_____

Name: _____   Date: _____

Associating Words with Feelings

Language Literacy Lessons / Words & Vocabulary Elementary
Copyright ©2002 by Incentive Publications, Inc.
Nashville, TN.

Greetings

The nicest greeting cards are cards that are made by hand for a special person. Match words and phrases from the two columns below to make messages to send for each of the occasions listed. Write each message on the line next to the appropriate occasion.

Sending . . .   . . . concern
May this be . . .   . . . happy thoughts
Please accept . . .   . . . the best one yet
Sincere . . .   . . . special wishes
Thinking . . .   . . . congratulations
Offering . . .   . . . you well
Wishing . . .   . . . my appreciation

BIRTHDAY. _____

THANKYOU. _____

ANNIVERSARY. _____

ILLNESS. _____

HOLIDAY. _____

FRIENDSHIPS. _____

SYMPATHY. _____

Name: _____   Date: _____   55

Language Literacy Lessons / Words & Vocabulary Elementary
Copyright ©2002 by Incentive Publications, Inc.
Nashville, TN.

Associating Words with Feelings

How Would You Feel?

Under each picture, write a sentence telling how you would feel if you were the person in the picture.

When you have finished, color the pictures.

_____

_____

_____

_____

_____

_____

_____

_____

_____

_____

_____

_____

Date:

Associating Words with Feelings

Language Literacy Lessons / Words & Vocabulary Elementary
Copyright ©2002 by Incentive Publications, Inc.
Nashville, TN.

Double Letters Are Better

While their friends watch television programs, Benny and Barry play word games. Their favorite game is named "Double Letters Are Better."

Here are the rules for their game.

Help them select words with double letters from the word box to complete sentences for the game.

Word Box						
football	good	jelly	hello	eggs	dollar	cookies
feet	mall	coffee	tree	door	books	boots

1. Benny chooses jam, but not _____.
2. Barry likes _____ with ham.
3. Benny and Barry both like _____ better than tea.
4. Benny asked Barry to close the _____ and open he window.
5. Barry asked his mother to bake _____ for his birthday rather than a cake.
6. Benny uses his hands more than he uses his _____.
7. Barry asked Benny to meet him at the _____ instead of the park.
8. Benny says "hi," but Barry always says "_____."
9. Barry asked for four quarters rather than a _____ bill.
10. Barry stood behind the _____ in front of the house.
11. Benny chooses the comics while Barry reads _____.
12. Barry likes sandals better than _____.
13. Barry's favorite game is hockey, while Benny likes _____.
☆. 14. Both Benny and Barry say it is _____ to obey school rules and bad to disobey the teacher.

Language Literacy Lessons / Words & Vocabulary Elementary
Copyright ©2002 by Incentive Publications, Inc.
Nashville, TN.

Exhibiting Word Sensitivity

Hot or Cold

This igloo was built with "cold" words.
Warm it up by adding "hot" words.

Use some of the words to write a sentence describing the igloo.

_____

_____

ice

cold

freeze

blizzard

frozen

chilly

cool

snow

icicles

frosty

nippy

Name: _____   Date: _____

Forming Sensory Impressions

Language Literacy Lessons / Words & Vocabulary Elementary
Copyright ©2002 by Incentive Publications, Inc.
Nashville, TN.

List-Maker's Lists

Write 5 words for each word list below.
The first one has been done for you.

1. sad
2. happy
3. lonely
4. friendly
5. angry

1. _____
2. _____
3. _____
4. _____
5. _____

1. _____
2. _____
3. _____
4. _____
5. _____

1. _____
2. _____
3. _____
4. _____
5. _____

Now make up two word lists of your own.

1. _____
2. _____
3. _____
4. _____
5. _____

1. _____
2. _____
3. _____
4. _____
5. _____

Name: _____   Date: _____

Language Literacy Lessons / Words & Vocabulary Elementary
Copyright ©2002 by Incentive Publications, Inc.
Nashville, TN.

Forming Sensory Impressions

Consonant Characters

Write a silly consonant story to fit each of the characters below.

In each story, use as many words as possible that begin with the same letter that begins the character's name.

Billy Bubbles

Billy Bubbles blows better bubbles than Betty Berry or Bart Brown.

He brings bread and butter for breakfast and beef and beans for lunch.

Sad Sam

_____

_____

_____

_____

Playful Patty

_____

_____

_____

_____

Name: Date:

Forming Sensory Impressions

Language Literacy Lessons / Words & Vocabulary Elementary
Copyright ©2002 by Incentive Publications, Inc.
Nashville, TN.

Picture This

First mate Blake had a habit of writing in his journal.

He especially likes to use idioms because their meaning is different from what the words actually say.

Beside each idiom Blake recorded in his journal, draw a picture to show what it would look like if the words meant what they said.

1. It was raining cats and dogs.

4. I tried, but failed, to hold my tongue.

2. The sea was as quiet as a mouse.

5. I had one more trick up my sleeve.

3. The captain really gets in my hair.

6. He put his foot in his mouth again.

Name: _____

Language Literacy Lessons / Words & Vocabulary Elementary
Copyright ©2002 by Incentive Publications, Inc.
Nashville, TN.

Interpreting Figurative and
Idiomatic Expressions

Say it Another Way

Good writers are constantly looking for new and different words to use to make their writing more interesting.

Select two words from the word box to replace each of the words below.

Add one of your own to each list. Use your thesaurus if you need help.

Word List:

injure	conceal	originate	harm
boring	tiny	disguise	elderly
ancient	begin	uninteresting	small

hurt _____

_____

dull _____

_____

old _____

_____

hide _____

_____

little _____

_____

start _____

_____

Name: _____

Date: _____

Interpreting Sensations Suggested by Words

Language Literacy Lessons / Words & Vocabulary Elementary
Copyright ©2002 by Incentive Publications, Inc.
Nashville, TN.

A Jumping Riddle

What animal comes from Australia, jumps all about, and has a full pouch?
Fill in the letters to find out.

A = 1   C = 3   E = 5   G = 7   I = 9   K = 11 M = 13 O = 15 Q = 17 S = 19 U = 21 W = 23 Y = 25
B = 2   D = 4   F = 6   H = 8   J = 10 L = 12 N = 14 P = 16 R = 18 T = 20 V = 22 X = 24 Z = 26

$\overline{1}$ $\overline{13}$ $\overline{15}$ $\overline{20}$ $\overline{8}$ $\overline{5}$ $\overline{18}$

$\overline{11}$ $\overline{1}$ $\overline{14}$ $\overline{7}$ $\overline{1}$ $\overline{18}$ $\overline{15}$ $\overline{15}$

$\overline{23}$ $\overline{9}$ $\overline{20}$ $\overline{8}$

$\overline{20}$ $\overline{8}$ $\overline{18}$ $\overline{5}$ $\overline{5}$

$\overline{2}$ $\overline{1}$ $\overline{2}$ $\overline{9}$ $\overline{5}$ $\overline{19}$

Write action words to tell 10 more things the animal can do:

1. _____
2. _____
3. _____
4. _____
5. _____
6. _____
7. _____
8. _____
9. _____
10. _____

Name: _____ Date: _____ (63)

Language Literacy Lessons / Words & Vocabulary Elementary
Copyright ©2002 by Incentive Publications, Inc.
Nashville, TN.

*Interpreting Sensations and Moods
Suggested by Words*

Who is Ms. Name To-Do-Lo?

An adjective is a word that describes or gives a clearer picture of a noun.

Meet Ms. Name To-Do-Lo. She lives on a cold mountaintop in a faraway land.

Write an adjective on each of her spots to tell about her.

Name:

Date:

Recognizing and Using Descriptive Words

A Scary Trail

To find your way out of the scary house, follow the scary word trail.
Use a word from the word list to finish each sentence.

Words to use:

sick   frightened   terrified   embarrassed

afraid   alarmed

scared

When a car I am riding in starts to skid on the street I am ....

When someones tells me a scary story, I am ....

When a stray dog starts to chase my bike, I am ....

When everyone in my class except me understands a joke, I feel ....

When I smell smoke coming from the hallway, I am ....

START HERE

When I hear strange noises in the middle of the night, I am ....

QUICK! escape!

Name: Date:

Language Literacy Lessons / Words & Vocabulary Elementary
Copyright ©2002 by Incentive Publications, Inc.
Nashville, TN.

Recognizing and Using Descriptive Words

A Step Ahead

Stay a step ahead of the animals by crossing out every other letter on the path, beginning with the second letter.

Write the names of the animals as you meet them. Beside each animal's name, write just one word that could be used to describe the animal.

START

E D L S E U

S G X T E N C A B H G P U

I T R O A L F P F Y E H

T M N L O K I J L

N I O G P E L R B S J

A P N

A C K O E M A Q P X E Y

Z

U B L E I

R H A F L R E B O U P S A V R W D

1. _ _ _ _ _ _ _ _ _   _ _ _ _ _ _
2. _ _ _ _ _ _ _ _ _   _ _ _ _ _ _
3. _ _ _ _ _   _ _ _ _ _ _
4. _ _ _ _ _ _   _ _ _ _ _ _

5. _ _ _ _ _ _ _ _   _ _ _ _ _ _
6. _ _ _ _   _ _ _ _ _ _
7. _ _ _ _ _ _   _ _ _ _ _ _
8. _ _ _ _ _ _ _ _   _ _ _ _ _ _

Which jungle animal would you **least** like to meet face to face in the jungle?

_____

Name: _____   Date: _____

Recognizing and Using Descriptive Words

Language Literacy Lessons / Words & Vocabulary Elementary
Copyright ©2002 by Incentive Publications, Inc.
Nashville, TN.

Color and Write

Try to use every crayon or colored marker you have to color this picture.
Write 1 sentence to describe the butterfly.
Write 1 sentence to describe the flowers.
Write 1 sentence to describe the trees.

_____

_____

_____

_____

_____

_____

Name: _____

Date: _____

Language Literacy Lessons / Words & Vocabulary Elementary
Copyright ©2002 by Incentive Publications, Inc.
Nashville, TN.

Recognizing and Using Descriptive Words

Interesting Characteristics

Look carefully at each person pictured below.

Give each person a name.
Write 3 characteristics which describe each person.
Write what you think each person's hobby might be.

1. _____ (name)

_____

_____

_____

HOBBY: _____

2. _____ (name)

_____

_____

_____

HOBBY: _____

3. _____ (name)

_____

_____

_____

HOBBY: _____

4. _____ (name)

_____

_____

_____

HOBBY: _____

Name: _____   Date: _____

Recognizing and Using Descriptive Words   *Language Literacy Lessons / Words & Vocabulary Elementary*

A Silly Story

Fill each of the critters below with descriptive words.
Then select one of the critters to write a silly story about. Use all your descriptive words in the story.
Give your story the best possible title to tell the reader what the story is about.

_____

_____

_____

_____

_____

_____

_____

_____

_____

_____

Name: _____   Date: _____ 69

Recognizing and Using Descriptive Words

Explain It

Draw a picture of an unusual animal or an animal in an unusual setting.
Color the picture.
Write 9 words that describe the animal. Use the words in a
paragraph to explain to someone exactly what the animal looks like.

Word List:

1. _____
2. _____
3. _____

4. _____
5. _____
6. _____

7. _____
8. _____
9. _____

_____

_____

_____

_____

_____

_____

Name: _____   Date: _____

Recognizing and Using Descriptive Words   *Language Literacy Lessons / Words & Vocabulary Elementary*
Copyright ©2002 by Incentive Publications, Inc.
Nashville, TN.

No Dictionary, Please

Select any one letter of the alphabet.

Without using a dictionary, try to write 20 words that begin with the letter.

1. _____   11. _____
2. _____   12. _____
3. _____   13. _____
4. _____   14. _____
5. _____   15. _____
6. _____   16. _____
7. _____   17. _____
8. _____   18. _____
9. _____   19. _____
10. _____   20. _____

It would be fun to ask a friend to do this with you.
Using the same letter, race to see who can write 20 words first.

If you simply can't think of 20 words, after giving it a good try, use your dictionary for help.

Name: _____   Date: _____

How's Your Word Knowledge?

Read this story carefully.
Then answer the questions below.

1. One day in the middle of our trip, we agreed to go sightseeing. **2.** We split into 3 groups and decided to meet at the car at 5:00 p.m.. **3.** At 3:00 p.m. I had already forgotten where the car was. **4.** "Let's see if we can find the car," I said to my older brother. **5.** We walked around until we saw familiar sights. **6.** "It's just around this corner," my brother said. **7.** "I know— great!" I said. **8.** We turned the corner, but the car wasn't there. **9.** "Has the car disappeared, or are we lost?" I asked.

1. Circle the word that could best be used to take the place of "agreed" in sentence 1.

    decided   argued   thought

2. Circle the word that means almost the same thing as "split" in sentence 2.

    divided   joined   remained

3. Circle the word that means the opposite of "forgotten" as it is used in sentence 3.

    guessed   slipped   remembered

4. Circle the phrase that best explains what "familiar" means in sentence 5.

    we had seen them before
    we never had seen them
    we didn't know whether we had seen them

5. Circle the word that explains how the person who is telling the story feels at the end.

    happy   confused   hungry

Demonstrating Word Knowledge   *Language Literacy Lessons / Words & Vocabulary Elementary*
Copyright ©2002 by Incentive Publications, Inc.
Nashville, TN.

Travel the Word Highway

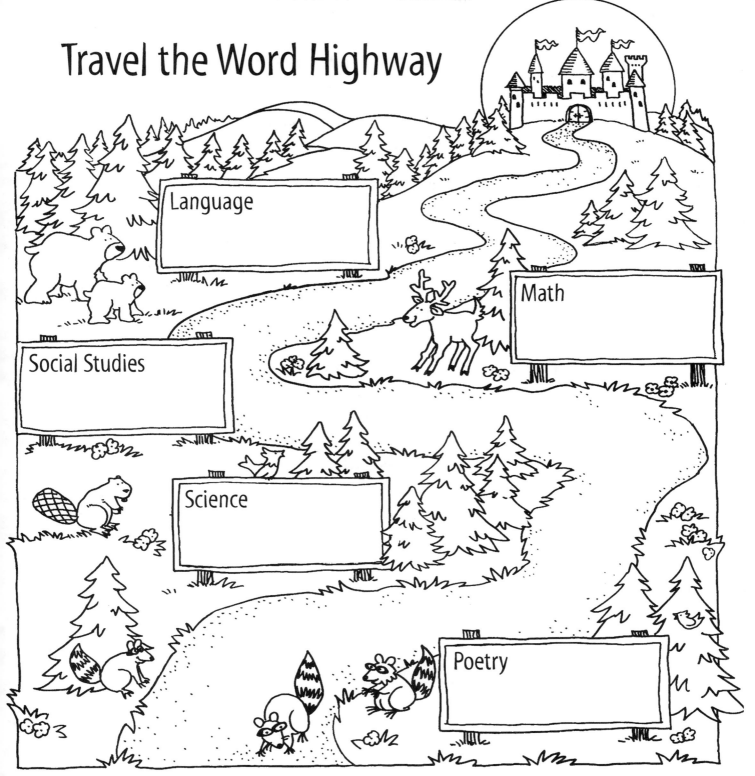

Language

Math

Social Studies

Science

Poetry

Be a word collector. Look in your textbooks or a reference book for very unusual words about these subjects.

Look for words that you do not know.

Collect a word and its meaning to write on each sign.

Name: _____   Date: _____   (73)

Language Literacy Lessons / Words & Vocabulary Elementary   *Exhibiting Word Appreciation Skills*

Construction Crew

All newspaper reporters know that every news article should include information on who, when, where, why, and what happened when covering a story. The best reporters hold their readers' attention by adding enough descriptive words or phrases to give the writing "pizzazz."

Each of these sentences tells something that happened to someone. In other words, you have the "who" and the "what." Add one word or phrase from each column below to make these simple, unexciting sentences more interesting. Use each word or phrase only once.

Where	When	"Pizzazz"
on another planet	last Sunday	bewitching
at the beach	on the stroke of 12	gorgeous
on a city street	just before dark	magnificent
at the cave's entrance	a year ago today	hideous
in the garden	yesterday	unrealistic
at the museum	last week	glamorous
over the rainbow	at dawn	heartbreaking

1. She bought the blouse.

_____

2. We saw the sunset.

_____

3. I lost my kite.

_____

4. He heard that screech.

_____

5. Mother smelled a rose.

_____

6. The girl's tears fell.

_____

7. She heard the news.

_____

Exhibiting Word Appreciation Skills   *Language Literacy Lessons / Words & Vocabulary Elementary*
Copyright ©2002 by Incentive Publications, Inc.
Nashville, TN.

Appendix

Answer Key

Page 12

Words to be capitalized:

1. Jean's	8. Mike
2. Debbie	9. Margaret
3. Monty, Statue, Liberty	10. Emily's
4. Mrs., Streams, Brook, St.	11. Thanksgiving, Day
5. Julie's	12. December
6. Blake	13. Tuesday
7. Noun Town	14. African
	15. Postal, United

Page 13

Letters colored yellow:

D, F, T, C, G, H, K, N, P, R, S, X, R, W, M,

Letters colored orange: A, U, E O, I

Be sure students have circles the long U sounds in the following words:

Ursula, Upchurch, under, umbrella, until, uncle, unpacked, unused, and ukulele.

Page 14

Corrected paragraphs should read:

If you work carefully, you can find the missing consonants right under Sly Sam the Sleuth's eyes. Circle a consonant when you put it in its proper place, and you will know not to go looking for it again.

Sly Sam has been assigned to the Great Consonant Case. Consonants keep disappearing in large numbers right out of otherwise sensible sentences. More consonants are missing every day. The words are beginning to panic, and though Sly Sam is smart and brave, even he is desperate. Can you come to his rescue?

Please hurry and replace the missing consonants to return peace and quiet to Sly Sam's world.

Special Message from Sam: "Thanks!"

Page 15

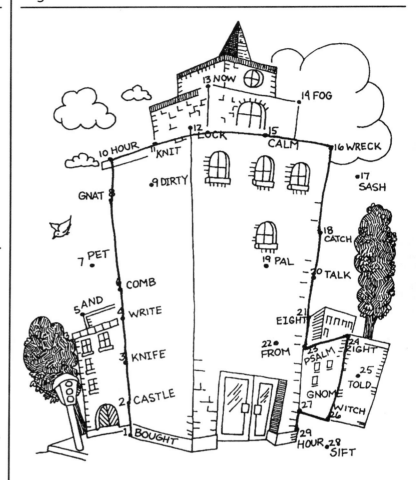

Page 17

Double-Letter "ing" Words:	Dropped-Letter "ing" Words:
hopping	coming
grinning	waking
planning	snoring
tapping	timing
sitting	striking
swimming	living
fanning	loving
trimming	hoping
batting	liking

Answer Key

Page 18

The correct passage reads:

Finding hidden treasure is not an easy task.

We searched a long time before spotting the first one.

Suddenly we saw the opened chest full of brilliant gems resting on the ocean's floor.

Jewels and gems of every description appeared before our eyes.

Quickly, we rushed straight ahead to claim the chest.

Imagine our surprise when the chest failed to move when we pushed and pulled with all our strength.

In spite of our mighty moves, the chest remained in its original position.

Straining every muscle in our body we tried lifting the chest upright.

Alas, our efforts were in no way successful.

That chest filled with treasures untold was there to stay.

Page 19

Phonetic Translation:
> You don't need a ruler
> To translate this fooler
> Just use all you know
> About phonics and GO!

Page 23

Check to be sure students have linked words and pictures appropriately.

Page 24

1-syllable words colored green:
Full, One, Who, Truth, Bit, Rot, Like, Act

2-syllable words colored orange:
Action, Early, Balloon, Gallop, Struggle, Visit, Bacon, Carrot, Pony, Panic, Twinkle, Fifty, Windy, Tennis, Bundle

3-syllable words colored brown:
Pottery, Dangerous, Happiness, Tiresome, Director, Property

Page 25

hour = hr.	December = Dec.
Drive = dr.	Centimeter = cent.
Wednesday = Wed.	Pound = lb.
Year = yr.	Avenue = Ave.
Doctor = Dr.	Yard = yd.
Mister = Mr.	Kilogram = kilo.
Feet = ft.	Road = rd.
Paid = pd.	Minute = min.
Inch = in.	February = Feb.
Sunday = Sun.	Liter = lt.
Mile = mi.	

Page 26

did not = didn't	is not = isn't
have not = haven't	you are = you're
we are = we're	let us = let's
that is = that's	should not = shouldn't

Page 27

I/will = I'll	Was/not = wasn't
Does/not = doesn't	Where/is = where's
Could/not = couldn't	We/will = we'll
You/will = you'll	You/are = you're
They/are = they're	Has/not = hasn't
We/are = we're	They/will = they'll
I/am = I'm	Was/not = wasn't
She/will = she'll	Would/not = wouldn't
Were/not = weren't	Has/not = hasn't
Can/not = can't	Have/not = haven't
There/is = there's	Should/not = shouldn't

Page 29

1. fish or hook	7. butter or fly
2. note or book	8. step or ladder
3. straw or berry	9. foot or ball
4. tea or kettle	10. coat or tail
5. screw or driver	11. ink or stand
6. chalk or board	

Answer Key

Page 33

Words that don't belong:

1. Penny	8. Ball
2. Pat	9. Bag
3. Top	10. Rack
4. Hot	11. Strip
5. Three	12. Bring
6. Strip	13. Shop
7. Litter	14. Tale

Circled Plurals:

1. Pencils	8. Bells
2. Pans	9. Bugs
3. Toes	10. Rocks
4. Hats	11. Straps
5. Trees	12. Strings
6. Stops	13. Ships
7. Letters	14. Tails

Page 34

Bear — Bears	Goat — Goats
Calf — Calves	Rooster — Roosters
Deer — Deer	Fox — Foxes
Fly — Flies	Sparrow — Sparrow
Giraffe — Giraffes	Dove — Doves
Goose — Geese	Elephant — Elephants
Mouse — Mice	Butterfly — Butterflies
Sheep — Sheep	Octopus — Octopuses
Wolf — Wolves	Tiger — Tigers

Page 30

Page 37

1. well
2. visit
3. visit
4. cold
5. cold
6. well
7. Answers will vary.

Page 40

Words crossed out:
   Potato
   Celery
   Spinach
   Pear
   Lemon

Page 41

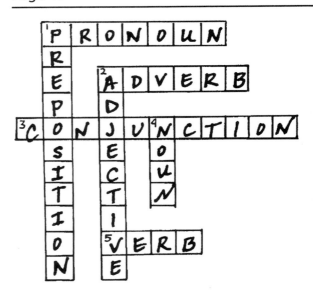

Page 42

Category answers may vary slightly.

1. cross out: shorts
   category: cold weather clothes

2. cross out: parrot
   category: food

Language Literacy Lessons / Words & Vocabulary Elementary
Copyright ©2002 by Incentive Publications, Inc.
Nashville, TN.

Answer Key

3. cross out: lily
   category: animals
4. cross out: chalk
   category: reference books
5. cross out: poncho
   category: dwellings
6. cross out: apple
   category: vegetables
7. cross out: growing
   category: weather
8. cross out: New York City
   category: countries
9. cross out: bucket
   category: units of measure

Page 45

1. whistled
2. Circled words: wintry, wind, icy, storm
3. deceased
4. living
5. poured
6. noisily
7. frightened
8. Underline: "A driving rain poured"
9. eerie
10. earth
11. yellow
12. attempted
13. eroding
14. forward
15. forbidding and sullen
16. mellow

Page 50

Answers may vary slightly.

1. dirty	6. behind	11. dark
2. light	7. tall	12. stingy
3. happy	8. big	13. frown
4. cold	9. cowardly	14. day
5. top	10. sharp	15. slow

Page 53

1. wand	4. wall	7. notebook
2. crown	5. dancing	8. fork
3. croak	6. goose	9. sun

Page 56

1. ate = eight	9. not = knot
2. bare = bear	10. pale = pail
3. be = bee	11. pare = pear
4. bough = bow	12. sale = sail
5. carat = carrot	13. tee = tea
6. dough = doe	14. tow = toe
7. heir = hair	15. thrown = throne
8. flour = flower	

Page 57

1. jelly	5. cookies	9. dollar	13. football
2. eggs	6. feet	10. tree	14. good
3. coffee	7. mall	11. books	
4. door	8. hello	12. boots	

Page 62

Answers will vary.

Page 63

Answer to riddle: A Mother Kangaroo with Three Babies

Page 64

Answers will vary.

Page 65

Answers will vary.

Page 66

1. Elephant	3. Lion	5. Snake	7. Zebra
2. Giraffe	4. Tiger	6. Ape	8. Leopard

Page 72

1. decided	4. we had seen them before
2. divided	5. confused
3. remembered	